AESOP THE STORYTELLER
A Book of Fables Retold in Verse

AESOP THE STORYTELLER
A Book of Fables Retold in Verse

by
Leon Conrad

Illustrated by
Alessandro Scafi

Published by
Aladdin's Cave

First published in Great Britain in 2007 by
Aladdin's Cave Publishing
31 Ryfold Road, Wimbledon Park London, SW19 8DF
Second edition published in 2024
aladdinscavepublishing@gmail.com

ISBN 978-0-9556391-8-0

A catalogue record for this book is available from the British Library.

1 3 5 7 9 10 8 6 4 2

Printed in Great Britain

Written in 2006 and 2007
to Commemorate
the 200th Anniversary
of the Act of the Abolition of Slavery

Dedicated to Katya,
whose inspiration and helpful suggestions
I very much appreciate

FOREWORD

These stories started out being spun from thin air
By a fellow called Aesop in a big market square.
This was way before Remus, La Fontaine or Voltaire;
Before Luther used these stories in sermons and
prayer.
Now you won't find one moral printed here in this book
And it just doesn't matter how hard you look.
I'm sorry if you think I've taken them away –
I haven't. It's how Aesop told them way back in his day.
He wanted to help people think matters through
For themselves. There's no way he – or I –
          would presume to tell you
What you should think about what's right or wrong.
You'll find your own truths in them before long.
So awaken your mind and lend me an ear –
Come, free your senses. I'll take you to where
There's a magical place, filled with creatures with flair;
A country of wolf, sheep, of crow, stork and bear,

Of talking trees, rabbits,
the fox in his lair –
The power of these stories
will take us right there.
Leon Conrad, London, March 2007

TABLE OF CONTENTS

The Fox and the Grapes

In a time beyond our time,
In a land beyond our land,
A fox,
A brown fox,
    A young fox,
        A young, brown fox,
          A naughty fox –
A fox who was used to getting what he wanted
    And getting what he wanted exactly when he
        wanted it,
    A fox who was used to taking what he wanted,
    Whether others wanted him to or not
        (Usually they didn't) – is sniffing the air.
This fox –
        Today –
This young, brown fox
        Today –
This naughty fox –
        Today –
Is HUNGRY!

He's wandering about
    Wanting to seek out
    A tasty snack
        To take right back
          To his lair
            To enjoy there.
But there isn't much about.

No matter where he sticks his snout
    He cannot sniff a morsel out.
He cannot find a single thing
    That he feels would really bring
        Him satisfaction … until …

A whiff of something in the breeze ...
    It isn't rabbit ...
    Isn't cheese ...
He turns a corner ... and there ...
    Supported on a cane,
        (The smell is driving him insane)
          He sees …

Grapes!

And says,

"WANT them!
WANT those grapes.
DIG those grapes
And their groovy shapes.

The sight of them makes
My eyes go weepy
Just let me … creeeepy … creeeeepy ...
Up … to … them.
Their mottled bloom
Just makes me swoon.
Hanging on the vine,
Looking just DIVINE.
(Shame to waste on wine.)
I'd be doing them a favour –
Just imagine all that flavour!
Mmm … my favourite – Merlot!
What a find – and what a show!
A splendid vine –
Found just in time
For me to satisfy my hunger!
They look so sweet
They'll be good to eat.
A succulent treat –
But … to reach them will require a feat
Of dexterity and skill
Which will demand all my will-

Power and control.
Oh … be still my soul!"
… He licks his lips,
Stretches up, balancing on the tips
Of his hind claws,
But try as he might,
Those grapes stay in sight –
But well out of reach.
He circles the vine,
Hoping to dine
On the fruit,
Carry off the loot.
He starts clawing at the stakes,
"Oh, come on, grapes,
Wontcha hang a little lower,
Just an ittie bittie lower,
Just for me?"

A passing mouse,
Observing fox's pains,
His straining, bulging veins,
Says to him,
 *"You'll have to go hungry!"*

That makes the fox angry.
He thinks it's absurd
That a mouse should be heard
Having the last word.
He says with a glower,
"Those grapes? They're all SOUR."
He goes off,
Feeling dour,
HUNGRY,
Sad,
But also glad
He's had the last word.
Is that so absurd?

Whether or not it's absurd,
It's the way of the world.

The Lion and the Mouse

In a field of corn,
Birds chirping,
Bees humming …

"Seventeen … Eighteen …
Nineteen … twenty …
Ready or not, I'm coming."
The field mouse thinks as he runs to and fro,
'Now where did all the others go?'
"Found one!
          Found two!
                    Found you!
                              And you!

One more to find … where can he be?
    Maybe up here …
              I'll just go and see."

And he climbs up a ridge in that yellow field of corn
Where the sun-kissed ground feels soft and warm

Doesn't feel like ground.
Doesn't smell like corn.
Feels too soft.
Looks too yellow.
The mouse is on a hill.

But the hill is not a friendly fellow!

The hill – it moves.
It stands up tall.
And that very small mouse
Squeaks, "Eek! I'm going to fall!"

He loses his grip, thinks,
'I'm going to trip!'
'My time has come.'
His heart beats louder
Than a kettle drum.
Then he hears a sound –
Four score and forty-four
Bold brass trumpets aren't louder
Than that dreadful sound –
A roar that echoes
   round and round
   As the mouse falls down
   Towards the ground, then …
      Stops … before he hits the floor,
      Caught fast within … a lion's paw.

    Oh-oh!

    Poor, poor, poor mouse!

You'd think that mouse
Would have died of fright –
But he thought, 'I might as well
Put up a fight.'
So he drew himself up to his full height,
As the lion brought him closer to his teeth pearly white –
"Mr Lion," he squeaks, "Don't eat me tonight.
You're known to be nice. You're known to be good.
That's why you're king of the beasts in the wood.
What good will it do if you eat me today?
Forgive me, please – I just went astray.
I was playing hide and seek with my friends down there
And I really don't know how I ended up in your hair!
Please let me go. Please let me go and play.
You never know – I might be useful to you one day.
The lion laughs! But feels the mouse's words pierce
His heart, which was normally bold and fierce.
And he growls, "OK, little mouse – I'll let you go."
And he puts the mouse down – the mouse bows low.
He thanks the lion, who roars, "Off you go!"

The mouse ne'er forgets the lion's kindness that day
And he and his friends play the summer away.
Then one autumn day
As they play in the hay,
They hear a lion roar
From quite far away,

"Help me! I'm caught. I'm tied up in string!
I've tried all I can – can't get out of this thing!

How will I ever get out of this fix?
I'm not ready to die – I'm not even six!"

The mouse knows the lion is caught in a net
And cries,
    "Don't worry, I'll save you yet.
    There's no way I'll let them treat you like a pet –
    Put you in a zoo – make a fool of you –
    Put you in a circus act ...
    And that's a fact!"

He gathers up some mice
They reach the lion in a trice.
As soon as they get there,
They start chewing on the snare.
The lion says, "Boy, am I glad to see you!"
Soon the ropes they've bitten through.

The lion breaks free.
Feels no more misery.

And he lives on happily
For a very long time after,
Sharing with his rodent friends
Both tears and laughter.

The Fable of the Stag

In forest green,
    where rivers flow,
A stag ran free,
Like you and me –
In forest green,
    where rivers flow.
And sun pours through the leaves … so slow
It makes our stag go, 'Hmmm …
I think I'd like a little drink …'.
And so –
Well, off he goes,
    like this:
        just so ...
To drink from the great broad sapphire lake
Right at the heart of the forest green,
Where fish glide slowly in between
The sun-kissed lotuses serene.
Our stag, he dips his head, sticks out his tongue
And takes a sip – [slurp] sip one –
[slurp] sip two – [slurp] and three – [slurp] and four –
Then … pauses.

The water clears.
'What's that I see?
Can that … strange thing … be ME?

What massive horns – I sure like them.
They make me look wise.
I never would condemn their size,
Their weight, their noble scale –
My legs, well, that's another tale.
They're spindly, wiry, thin, and scrappy ...'.
Well, he just thought them plain old ...
No, even worse –

But I won't put those words into verse!
Let's say the thought of them made him unhappy.
He couldn't move his eyes away –
He was prouder than a peacock – it had made his day.
So there he lingered, admiring his antlers;
  pawing the ground,
Never noticing a tell-tale sound –
The crack of a twig that echoed round
And then another –
It wasn't his mother.
It wasn't his brother.

WHIZZ!

The arrow shoots right past his ear.
The stag rears up, impelled by fear,
And just takes off,
Galloping through the trees
Whipping up a breeze
Panting, ill at ease,
Rushing through the trees,
Racing through the trees,

Faster, faster through the trees –
Behind him, hounds bark,
Hunters chasing,
Driving him deeper,
Deeper,
Into the wood …
Pushing,
Panting,
Ranting,
Racing,
Stuck!
Can't move further –
He's trapped!
Heart racing …
Antlers caught …
Can't break the branches …

Panic …

'Should have known my speedy legs
Were worth more than
My horrid horns.'
He begs to see another day –
Tries to get free –

Too late.

But wait –
Perhaps he will get free.

Who knows?

The Lion and the Donkeys

A donkey, trim and thin roamed free
    among the flowers.
Whenever he wanted to do
      something, he did it.
Wherever he wanted to go, off he would leg it.
He grazed at will upon the green, green grass.
One day, he heard a sound – now, what should pass
Along a nearby road but another donkey,
Strong and sleek, hauling a heavy load,
Led by a man armed with a stick, who towed
Him on a rope tied round his muzzle.
Now why he would submit to that
Was quite a puzzle
To the donkey in the field.
His brain was sealed,
His thoughts congealed –
He couldn't figure it out at all.
Meanwhile, behind a nearby wall,

A Himalayan lion lurked.

(The lion's name was Brian.)
Don't ask me how he got there
Or why his name was Brian.
All I know is Brian was a very hungry lion.
He hadn't had enough to eat for days.
No breakfast, lunch or dinner
Meant Brian getting thinner ... thinner ... thinner.
Not good news – for him, or for the donkeys. Why?

If he got any thinner he'd go POP!

And the donkeys – well for them, that would be that.

Finito! Stop!

The wall was low (and no Berliner.)

      He peeped over the top

And thought, 'Gee – I am Lottery Winner!'

Two donkeys – but he could only go for one.

Which one would it be?

Donkey one, who's trim but thin?

Or strong, sleek donkey two? (He fancied him.)

His mouth was drooling.

His energy refuelling,

He crouched,

Dug his rear paws in the ground,

Weighed up his options,

Made a decision,

Prepared to leap –

And whoosh! Over the wall he went

      in one great bound.

In one straight line – and donkey … one found
Out … hey – he was the chosen one.
Not the nicest piece of meat on the menu,
But Brian, when all's said and done,
Didn't fancy a taste of the owner's stick upon his bum.
And so, the donkey
       with the heavy load

Lived on …
      to walk
          on

               down
                   the
                     road.

The Fox and the Crow

A tree grows near a castle in Bordeaux
Through which the breezes softly
come and go.

Upon that tree once perched a young black crow
When once a hungry fox stood down below.
Now the crow held in her beak a bit of cheese,
The smell of which made fox weak at the knees.
The fox was smart, and with a wily wink,
He said to himself, he said, 'Here's what I think:
Why go out and hunt, when here in front
Of me is a young black crow?
I wonder if the crow will go
And fall for my plan.
It's worth a try. It's time I began.'
He raised his head … and simply smiled.
The crow glanced down and was beguiled.
"Oh beautiful crow," fox said aloud,
The crow was clearly very wowed.
The fox oozed charm from every pore.
This way and that he paced the floor

And slowly started to turn up the heat
(Well … he was hungry and he wanted to eat.)
"Your eyes, like lanterns, in the darkest night,
Put fear to shame, put fright to flight,
And through your jet-black feathers lingering,
        the glow
Of sunlight lights up our world below.
You thrill me, fill me up with pure desire,
And when I look at you, my soul soars higher;
I hear your voice ring out over the birds' choir
And feel complete, replete, my greatest treat
To gaze upon your beauty as you tweet.
Please sing for me now, beauteous bird, that I
May bask in bliss just once before I die."
He turned his gaze upon the plain black bird –
His eyes were wet with tears, his vision blurred.
The crow was taken in by his request.
She took a breath in … puffed out her chest …
Lifted up her head, opened up her beak,
Expressed her soul in song – a dreadful squeak
Came out, which lasted far too long.

Down fell the cheese –
　　　　fox grabbed it quick and said,
"So long, my dear – I fear it is my duty
To let you know that while your brains do match
　　　　your beauty,
The voice that comes out from your throat –
If I were you, I'd get some lessons before I sang
　　　　another note."
The crow, dismayed, stopped short of a reprise,
Lamenting her sad loss of face – and cheese.
The fox went on his way, pleased with himself,
Leaving the crow feeling she could kill herself
And him – but didn't,
　　　　learned from the experience,
　　　　　　grew more wise,
And one day, in that place – surprise, surprise –
The same two creatures found themselves again,
And what was more surprising –
　　　　it was a replay of the scene!
For the crow had a new piece of cheese held fast within
Her beak.
　　　　They stopped, eyed one another up, and then,
Played out the scene for old time's sake again.

The fox he circled round, turned on the charm.

The crow looked on, without alarm.

His speech complete, she paused,

      she dipped her head,

She looked around …

      she placed the cheese inside a crack she'd found

Within the tree trunk just behind her back,

She preened her feathers, opened up her beak …

This time, no squawk, no quack, no squeak,

No grating noise emerged;

Instead, a sublime melody came out, that merged

Melodiously with the forest chorus,

A tuneful mix of notes of highest beauty.

Her voice was clear, her sound was fruity,

Sexy, sensual, sublime. In short, finer than fine.

The fox stood open-mouthed, so struck dumb with awe

That when she'd stopped,

      he couldn't even ask for more!

She flicked her tail feathers at him saucily,

Turned round, picked up the cheese,

      and flew off merrily.

For she'd gone off and taken singing lessons, see?

The fox went on his way, a humbled gent,
Both puzzled and confused at the event.
But that was not the last time that they met.
More years rolled by, and one fine summer's day,
When time had aged them both,
          their youthful vigour worn away,
They happened to be passing the same spot –
Now I know you may think it's a long, long shot –
But as rivers flow and gold gleams, this is true,
Guess what the crow had in her beak?
          Mmm hmmm – some Danish Blue.
They both looked older, weaker, thinner,
And both were ready for some dinner.
They looked at one another. And for old time's sake,
The fox resolved right there and then to make
A new start; to once and for all the hatchet bury
And composed a new verse
          in praise of his old adversary.
"Your eyes blaze bright – like stars in the night skies,
Providing hope when age fills us with sighs.
And though your jet-black feathers' youthful sheen is
          dimmed,

The splendour of your finery's still hymned
By connoisseurs of beauty far and wide.
In admiration and respect, I cast aside
All envy, all resentment ... I let go my pride,
And in humility, ask to hear your voice once again
wing
Out across the forest as you sing
Once more for me – so I may feel
My soul fly up to heaven, as you reveal
The inner beauty of your voice – however faded.
I hope my words, inadequate as they are,
            have now persuaded
You to sing for me, o beauteous bird, that I
May bask in bliss once more before I die."

A hint of sunlight flashed in the crow's moist eyes
As she slowly raised her head toward the skies
And consciously let fall the cheese within her beak,
Followed by a single tear …
            and with a voice cracked, weak,
Outlined the melody of memory from long ago
That floated hauntingly down to the fox below.
The fox then gently bit the cheese in two,
Took one half in his jaws, and then … withdrew.

The crow then glided down, picked up the rest.
And took it to the safety of her nest.

They never met again – well, not as far as I know,
But if you're ever visiting Bordeaux,
You'll recognise the tree there by the slow
Flow of the breezes through its branches,
Whispering the crow's song softly
As they come and go.

Wild Dog Dingo's Winter

It's freezing winter. Ice and snow
Cover the ground. Frost-tipped
Trees shudder off their snow shawls.

The tracks of the night-wanderers of the forest
Are criss-crossed by new-laid paths of claw and paw.
Icy, cold, shivering, wild dog Dingo curls up tighter,
Curved into a fur-frozen ball
Where nose, tail, paw join
To keep the heat in – keep the warmth in.
'Mmm – oh, to be in a warm place tonight …
Wouldn't take much to build a shelter –
A few planks of wood
Laid out neatly,
Not helter-skelter.
When summer comes,
That's what I'll do.'
And wild dog Dingo shiver-yawned and fell asleep,
Dreaming of a warmer space
A place of comfort,
Bliss and peace …

That saw him through the winter.

Then slowly, snow gives into spring,
And winter's grasp upon the land,
The trees, the snow clouds loosens
To let gentle showers of rain descend,
Through which the sun smiles
Rainbows
And life is worth living.
It's warming up,

And wild dog Dingo
Feels the soul-warming flutter
Of sunbeams meet his fur,
Inviting him to stretch out,
Uncurl his body –
Muscle, sinew, flesh, fur, bone unravel, loosen
And invite the sunbeams in
Beneath his fur;
Beneath his skin.
He stretches out, can hardly believe
He's grown so long.

'Admire my form, my shadow strong.
I'll never be able to build a home
That's big enough for me.
And anyway, it's far too warm.
I'll just lie here in ecstasy
And store the warmth right here inside.'

And so the days pass.

Sunshine turns the trees to red, then brown.

A leafy carpet covers up the ground

And forms a blanket Dingo snuggles up in.

And when winter comes again,

Freezing winter,

Wild dog Dingo,

In his chilly cradle, rocks himself to sleep,

Dreaming of the leaves

And the soul-kiss of the sun

And a warm place to snuggle up in;

While a frost-tipped tree above him

Shudders off its shawl of snow;

And on the ground, ice forms

Over layered snow;

And freezing winter almost stops time's flow –

Almost stops his breath.

And so, the seasons flow –

Even though here I must leave

Our story and that little,

Shivering, curled up ball of fur

Which is our wild dog Dingo.

The Fox and the Stork

A stork thought it would be great fun
To send his friend the fox an
　　invitation
To dine with him, and for his delectation
Prepared for him his favourite dish –
A most delicious broth of fish
Which he served up in what he had available:
A long-necked vessel, laid upon the floor –
　　he had no table.
(What can I say? He did what he was able.)

The fox arrived. He looked about.

He sniffed the vessel with his snout,

He circled it. His luck was out.

Out of his reach that broth would stay

He couldn't get to it, try as he may.

He tilted his head, stuck out his tongue,

He sucked, slurped, salivated, till kingdom come,

But not one drop of broth got to his tum.

Meanwhile, the stork, when it was his turn,

Stuck his beak into the long-necked urn

And sipped the broth up daintily.

The fox looked at him awkwardly,

Remembering his cousin who'd said wearily

The ripe grapes that he couldn't reach were sour

After he'd tried to get at them for well nigh near

      an hour.

This fox determined not to make the same mistake.

He swore he'd do his best for the stork's sake.

He went home hungry, had a meal at home,

The next day went to thank Jerome.

Jerome was the stork's name, you see.

"Thank you, Jerome, your soup smelt great,
I do decree. I'd love to see you (if you're free)
At next full moon. Do come for tea
At dusk beneath the old oak tree."
Jerome thought this idea delightful.
He went around those woods full
Of happiness and glee –
"Reynard's invited me to tea."
The fox's name was Reynard, see?

The moon grew thin, it disappeared,
Then in the dark sky reappeared;
It grew from crescent to half moon
And before they knew it, there it was – full moon

Jerome arrived at Reynard's door
And found, laid out upon the floor
The choicest food from Reynard's store
Arranged upon a wooden plate;
The smell – mmm hmmm – it was just great!
Jerome dipped in his dainty beak,
His manners suave, his movements chic,

But try as he might, vertical, oblique,
Straight on, or scooping up,
He couldn't schlurp one morsel up!

Reynard, however, enjoyed the meal.
For him, the vessel was ideal.
Each did the best they could;
Neither could do more.
That's how they were made.

Were the two left sore?
Or did they part friends?
Or was this a tale of sweet revenge?

The Wolf and the Kid

(or Doing What Comes Naturally)

A bright young lamb called Ralph
Looked around the dull but safe
Green field his flock was in
And said,
  "This place is boring.
    I want to go exploring."
So off he went … alone.
And on the way, he met
A hungry wolf called Brett –
Who took one look at him.
His smile stretched to a grin –
His lips he licked –
His brains he picked –
And set out to justify his kill.

Now Ralph was feeling thirsty,
And thought he'd have a tasty
Drink from a nearby stream.

And the wolf said,

"You've muddied this stream,
And now it's not clean.
And I can't drink from it."

"But …
I drank from down here.
The stream flows from up there …
So your bit can't be muddy."

"Well …
The grass that
you've been eating
While I was
up there sleeping
Wasn't yours to eat."

"But …
I've not had a thing.
I didn't even plan to begin
My meal."

"Well …
A year ago today,
You insulted me here.
So pay for it now."

"But …
How could I have done,
When I'm not even one
Year old yet?"

"Forget it, mate.
Prepare to meet your fate.
You're not going to make me wait
One more minute.
My tummy wants you in it,
And nothing you can say
Can make me change my mind.

I'll be kind. Relax. Unwind.
You won't feel a thing.
One bite and that's it – Ping!
Go 'Boo-hoo!'
I don't care.
What's that you say? Not fair?
That's a view that I don't share.

Now it's time for you to bid
The world goodbye.

I've enjoyed our brief discussion.
I do prefer young lamb to mutton.

Hello … er … Would you like some too?
Well, help yourself. Please do."

The Wolves, The Sheep and the Dogs

It was a time of war between the
    wolves and sheep;
A war so brutal it would make your mother weep.
The wolves were fierce and had the upper hand;
Their warriors were the strongest in the land.

But the sheep were cunning – even in their sleep
They planned and plotted, thinking how they'd creep
Up on the wolves and conquer them with tricks.
The wolves were then in quite a pretty fix.

The sheep poured glue upon the wolves
    when they were sleeping
And fought on sloping ground to keep them slipping,
Sliding, falling, tumbling, toppling, tripping;
But the wolves still fought on –
    gripping, nipping, ripping
The sheep to bits – grrraor, rawoor, raaah, raaaah!

The sheep then got the dogs to help them out.

That was a good move, without a doubt.

Those dogs were rough and wild –

     they had some clout!

The wolves said,

     "That's it. Let's not mess about.

     We'll call a truce – let's see if there's a way

     To stop the war and stop it from today."

One wolf spoke up (bit of a clever clogs.)

He said,

     "If we're not fighting, you won't need your dogs.

Let us look after them for you for a while.

We'll take them hostage. We'll treat them well, in style.

Provided you behave, they'll be okay.

It's the only way I can see to end this war today."

The dogs didn't mind, as long as they were fed.
The sheep agreed to what the wolf had said.
And with the dogs now safely out the way,
The wolves cried out, "Yippee! Hurrah! Hooray!"

In one fell swoop, they fell upon the sheep
And killed them all while they were still asleep.
The dying sheep: prostrate … dropping heart rate …
Realised how foolish they had been too late.

The Fox and His Tail

Hunter's on the prowl, and the fox
    don't know it.
Hunter's on the prow,l and the fox
    walks out.
Hunter's on the prowl, and the fox don't know it.
Hunter lays his traps, and then he's gone.

Traps are laid, and the fox don't know it.
Traps are laid, and the fox walks out.
Traps are laid, and the fox don't know it.
SNAP! goes a trap – his tail is gone!

Fox cries out in pain – "Ai-yai-yai-yai-yaiiiii!"
Fox cries out in pain 'cause his tail is gone.
Fox cries out in pain
    as he walks back through the forest.
Tail gone. Stump sore. Afraid and alone.

Fox calls a meeting to warn the other foxes.
Fox calls a meeting to tell them of his state.
Fox calls a meeting to warn the other foxes.
He knows they're going to laugh at him
but goes there anyway.

The foxes laugh when they see what he looks like.
The foxes laugh when they see his stump.
The foxes laugh when they see what he looks like.
Fox holds his head high. Inside, he just feels frail.

He lifts his head, saying, "Listen to me, brothers."
He lifts his head, saying, "Hear me out today."
He lifts his head, saying, "Listen to me, brothers.
I've really learned a thing or two since I lost my tail.

A tail's no use when hunters kill you for it.
A tail's no use if it slows you down too much.
A tail's no use when hunters hunt you for it.
And I think we'd all be better off without our bushy tails."

The foxes listen, growl as they discuss it.
The foxes listen. One says, "Hear me out, I pray."
The foxes listen, nod as he continues:
"You'd not be saying that if you had your tail today."

The laughter grows; the foxes jeer and mock him.
The laughter grows; the fox is sent away.
The laughter grows; the foxes jeer and mock him.
They all have tails, he doesn't.

     And what more can I say?

The Fox and the Ground Bird

There was a little bird
                that thought the best
Place she could build a comfy nest

Was on the solid ground,
And so she found
A safe and sheltered spot
Where she could squat.
            In her nest,
            She took a little rest
            And watched the world go by.

The plants nearby provided lots of food.
And if the bird was in the mood
To try some juicy worms,
The ground around
The nest was full of them –
The very best.

In her nest,
She looked out to the West
And watched the sun go down.

Now settled down at last in her abode,
The bird felt in a nesting mode.
She built a holly wall
To keep away
The creatures who might think
Of her as prey.

In her nest,
She felt that she was blessed
And watched the world go by.

She sat and preened her feathers one fine day
When who should come along that way …
Our dear old friend – yes,
Reynard, the sly fox,
Who thought, 'Ah ha!
Opportunity knocks!'
>In her nest,
>Bird felt a little stressed
>And glared as fox went by.

The fox said to the bird, "D'you want to play?
It would be so much fun today.
I promise not to eat you,
Yes I do.
Come, leave your nest and play.
Don't turn away."
>In her nest,
>With deeply felt unrest,
>Bird looked fox in the eye.

The bird flew up above the fox's head.
She coyly circled round … then said,
"Why, come up here then, sweetie.
In the sky.
Where clouds float freely by
Is where I'll stay –
  Stay and play
  Until you go away.
  'Cause here I know I'm safe."

Bird lived on past that day.
Fox sighed and turned away,
To seek another way
To fill his tummy.

The Merchant and the Mule

*(To be read in a jaunty anapaestic
or 'weak-weak-strong' rhythm)*
In a far-away town lived an
      entrepreneur, which just means
A smart guy who made money from starting up
   new business schemes –
      Schemes like selling the salt which he
   thought
         he'd get free from the sea.

For this scheme, the old man bought a mule and
   enough food and drink
For a trip which would take them three days, maybe
   four, I would think.
      After bidding farewell to his fam'ly,
        he took off to see

How much money he'd make selling sea salt
    back home in his town.
Now the road they took went past woods, orchards,
   a stream … and then down,

Down, down, down to the sea,
  where the merchant found there was no lack
 Of the salt which he planned to bring back …
  in a pack … on mule's back.

Once the pack was all loaded, he headed straight back
  up the slope.
He had watered and fed the mule well;
  the mule started to mope.
   The mule wasn't that pleased at the thought of
    the long journey back.
Not that used to the weight and unsure of its step,
  the mule tripped –
And the salt landed up in the stream,
  all because he had slipped.
   By the time he got out,
    half the salt had
     dissolved
      from the pack.

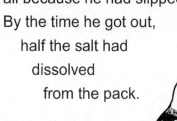

While the guy was upset, he decided he'd
    best be detached
And not count any chickens before any
    chickens had hatched.
        And the mule was delighted to find he'd a
            much lighter load
        Trotting happily on past the orchards and
        woods
            by the road.

When they got to the town, and the guy sold the salt
    he'd brought back,
He found out he'd still made enough money to
    give it a crack
        Once again – and so off they both went to the
            seaside to bring back more salt.

So once more past the woods, past the orchards, the
    stream and then down
To that quaint little old-fashioned seaside resort
    of a town,
        Then back homewards with salt. By the stream,
            the mule stopped … he just came to a halt!

Now this mule was no fool – he'd been up this 'ere
pathway before.
And he thought to himself,
'Why should I tote this load? It's a bore!'
So he tripped up and most of the salt ended up
in the stream.
The old merchant just couldn't believe it – he
wanted to scream!

Once they'd dried themselves off and recovered the
salt which remained,
And the merchant had scolded the mule, and
explained, and complained,
And arraigned and harangued him for
three days and nights on the road,

They both fin'lly got home where the man found it
wasn't that hard
To once more make a profit, but swore that he'd be
on his guard
Against any new tricks the mule thought might
diminish his load.

When once more they set out on the journey
    towards the blue sea,
The old mule thought, 'Now this is a whizz!'
    The man thought, 'Let's just see …'
        They arrived, and the man put a new load of
            stuff on the mule;
        As they set off back home, the mule thought,
            'Well, hey dude, this is cool!

I know just what I'll do when I pass that
    familiar place –
I'll slow down a bit, slip, try to slacken my pace
Then I'll stage a new fall – and my load
      will be very much less.'
The old merchant just led him back up
    the steep slope, well aware
Of the thought process going on
    under the mule's mane of hair.
When the mule did slip up, then recover,
    he found – can you guess?

Well, he didn't expect that his load would be
   heavier still!
The old merchant, he'd had it all planned –
   he'd decided to fill
      The mule's pack with large sponges
         that sucked up the water a treat
      So the mule found he'd loads more to carry
         when back on his feet!

'Cause the sponges sucked up lots of water you see
   from the stream …
And the mule learned his lesson …

... I tell you, this wasn't a dream,

For I heard it myself from the
   merchant's own mouth last weekend,

And on that note I'll wind up this fable –
   wait for it –

The END!

Postscript

I caught these fables floating on the air
And for your pleasure,
            wrapped them up in here.
So you can take them with you
Anywhere.

Go – tell these stories.
Read them,
Share them,
Enjoy them,
Set them free.
They are a gift … to all of you …
        from Aesop

and from me.

Treasures From Aladdin's Cave

Aladdin's Cave is a publishing house which specializes in the best in poetry, storytelling, and innovative combinations of print and audio books.

For news of new releases, contact aladdinscavepublishing@gmail.com

Printed in Great Britain
by Amazon